My First B...
ab...
Go...

Carine Mackenzie

CF4·K

10 9 8 7 6 5 4 3 2 1
© Copyright 2013 Carine Mackenzie
ISBN: 978-1-78191-276-8

Published by
Christian Focus Publications,
Geanies House, Fearn,
Ross-shire, IV20 1TW, Scotland, U.K.

The Scripture quotations in this book are based on the English Standard Version Anglicised.
Copyright © 2001 by Crossway Bibles, a division of Good News Publishers.

www.christianfocus.com
e-mail: info@christianfocus.com

Cover design by
Daniel van Straaten
All illustrations by Diane Mathes
Printed and bound by Bell and Bain, Glasgow.

MIX
Paper from
responsible sources
FSC® C007785

Contents

Introduction

The gospel is more than the story of Jesus that we read in Matthew, Mark, Luke and John. The good news – or gospel – is God's message to us about his Son, Jesus Christ, who died for sinners. Through repentance and faith in Him, sinners can be made right with God.

There are many definitions of the gospel in the Bible. The Bible is full of good news of God's salvation. By God's grace we believe the gospel and trust in Jesus Christ.

'For by grace you have been saved through faith. And this is not your own doing; it is the gift of God' (Ephesians 2:8).

May this little book help you to think about the gospel, to thank God for his gospel and to pass the good news on to someone else.

1. The Gospel is Good News

The beginning of the gospel of Jesus Christ, the Son of God.
Mark 1:1

Gospel means 'good news' – the good news about God's Son, Jesus Christ.

The good news is that Jesus Christ died for sinners. Those who repent and trust in him have their

sins forgiven and are made right with God. They receive the gift of eternal life.

Matthew, Mark, Luke and John wrote books which tell this message of Jesus or gospel.

The word **gospel** appears many times in the Bible.

We should thank God for this good news.

2. The Gospel Foretold

Paul ... set apart for the gospel of God, which he promised beforehand through his prophets in the holy Scriptures.
Romans 1:1-2

The gospel, or good news about the Saviour, was promised for a long time before Jesus was born. Jesus' defeat of the devil was hinted at in the Garden of Eden (Genesis 3:15).

Isaiah prophesied hundreds of years before it happened, that a child would be born who would be very special. His name would be Wonderful Counsellor, Mighty God, Everlasting Father, Prince of Peace. Micah foretold that the child would be born in Bethlehem. Many details of Jesus' life and death were prophesied in the Old Testament, and were fulfilled exactly.

God kept all his promises in Jesus Christ the Saviour.

3. The Saviour is Here

The angel said to them, 'Fear not, for behold, I bring you good news of great joy that will be for all the people. For unto you is born this day in the city of David a Saviour, who is Christ the Lord.'
Luke 2:10-11

An angel brought good news to the shepherds, telling them of the birth

of the Saviour. This was good news, not only for them, but for all people – good news for us today.

God the Son came to this world as a human baby, lived the perfect life here and died to pay the price for our sins.

God's plan of salvation for his people brings us great joy.

4. The Light of the Gospel

The god of this world has blinded the minds of the unbelievers, to keep them from seeing the light of the gospel of the glory of Christ, who is the image of God.
2 Corinthians 4:4

Jesus is our guiding light in this dark world. He said he is the light of the world. The gospel is like a light too

– guiding our path, giving us warmth and safety and help on our journey through life.

Darkness is very scary and dangerous. What good news that Jesus rescues us from that and gives us light.

5. The Gospel of Peace

As shoes for your feet ... put on
the readiness given by the gospel
of peace.
Ephesians 6:15

Jesus has promised to give us lasting
peace in our heart. Our sin gives us
a troubled conscience, a feeling of

unease, guilt and anxiety, knowing we are not right with God. We have peace with God through our Lord Jesus Christ when we trust in him.

6. The Gospel of Truth

Of this (hope) you have heard before in the word of truth, the gospel, which has come to you, as indeed in the whole world it is bearing fruit and growing.
Colossians 1:5-6

The words of the gospel of Jesus are true. Jesus himself is the truth that leads us to God.

False teachers will lead us astray to disaster. But the truth of the gospel will lead us safely on the journey of life to our final destination in heaven with the Lord Jesus.

7. The Gospel of the Kingdom

And this gospel of the kingdom will be proclaimed throughout the whole world as a testimony to all nations.
Matthew 24:14

A king is a ruler of a kingdom. There is a great kingdom made up of all God's people. Its ruler is Jesus Christ.

Jesus told several parables (or stories) to describe his kingdom. Although it may seem small and insignificant, it has a great effect and is very precious. The good news (gospel) of the kingdom will reach through the whole world. His kingdom can be found wherever there are people who trust and obey Jesus.

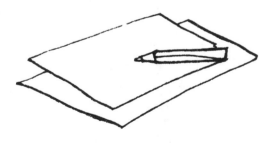

8. The Gospel of your Salvation

In him (Christ) you also, when you heard the word of truth, the gospel of your salvation, and believed in him, were sealed with the promised Holy Spirit.
Ephesians 1:13

How happy we are to hear news of someone being rescued from a

burning house or from the stormy sea. The best possible news is to know that we have been saved from the wrath and punishment that we deserve. We are brought from this danger by faith in Christ, to the safe place in God's love and favour. God, the Holy Spirit, helps us to appreciate just how wonderful the gospel of salvation is.

9. The Power of God

For I am not ashamed of the gospel, for it is the power of God for salvation to everyone who believes.
Romans 1:16

God has immense power – power to create the universe, to make a mountain and an elephant, to control the wind and the sea.

His power is shown above all in the conversion of a sinner. When Jesus died on the cross he defeated Satan, and showed his immense power over everything, even death, evil and Satan.

His immense power draws a sinner to love and trust him.

10. The Gospel in Five Words

Christ died for the ungodly.
Romans 5:6

This Bible verse has just five words, but what amazing good news. Everyone is a sinner, ungodly by nature. But in our weakness and sin, Christ Jesus died for us – not because we deserve it but because God decided. God is love.

11. The Debt is Paid

For I delivered to you as of first importance what I also received: that Christ died for our sins in accordance with the Scriptures.
1 Corinthians 15:3

Our sins deserve punishment from God. Sin has caused a great debt with God. But Jesus Christ has paid this debt for us when he died on the cross. The debt is cancelled. The price was too high for us to pay. Jesus paid for our sins with his own blood when it was shed on the cross.

12. The Lost is Found

**The Son of Man came to seek
and to save the lost.**
Luke 19:10

If you get lost, you feel so
frightened and anxious. You do not
know how to reach your destination.
You need help.

The good news of the gospel is that Jesus came to seek those who are lost and lead them to their destination – God's kingdom.

Jesus told us stories about a lost sheep, a lost coin and a lost son (Luke 15). When they were found, there was great celebration.

There is great joy in heaven when a lost sinner is found by Jesus Christ.

13. Sin is Cleansed

The blood of Jesus his (God's) Son cleanses us from all sin.
1 John 1:7

We have to regularly clean our bodies, our clothes and our homes to get rid of grime and dirt. But we cannot, by our own effort, get rid of the dirt and impurity that sin causes.

The good news of the gospel is that God cleanses us from all sin with the blood of Jesus. If we trust in Jesus, who shed his blood on the cross, we are made clean and acceptable in God's sight.

14. Forgiveness Forever

For I will forgive their iniquity, and I will remember their sin no more.
Jeremiah 31:34

If someone does something hurtful to us, we find it hard to forget. We often keep going back to think

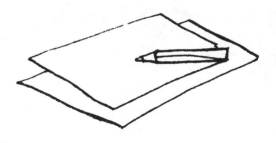

about the wrong done to us. God is not like us. He forgives us because of what the Lord Jesus has done on the cross. Our sin is covered – out of sight. God says he will remember it no more. Christ has dealt with it. This is good news.

Micah tells us that God will cast all our sins into the depths of the sea (Micah 7:19).

15. Freedom from Slavery

So if the Son sets you free, you will be free indeed.
John 8:36

Sin can capture our minds and hearts and make us slaves. Perhaps greed or jealousy or anger or dishonesty can hold a grip on our

life and keep us captive. Only Jesus can break these bonds and set us free from sin.

This is very good news. Jesus sets us free to a new life to serve God.

16. Found not Guilty

If anyone does sin, we have an advocate with the Father, Jesus Christ the righteous.
1 John 2:1

An advocate is a person who will speak for you to the judge in a court of law if you have done

something wrong. Our judge is God and we have all done many wrong things – by our actions, our words or our thoughts. These sins deserve God's punishment. But Jesus is our 'advocate' who pleads for us.

'He is able to save to the uttermost those who draw near to God through him, since he always lives to make intercession for them' (Hebrews 7:25).

17. God's Free Gift

For the wages of sin is death, but the free gift of God is eternal life in Christ Jesus our Lord.
Romans 6:23

The good news is that God has given us a free gift – totally undeserved - eternal life. We deserve death, but because of what the Lord Jesus has done we can receive the marvellous gift of eternal life.

Jesus told us that he came so that his people 'may have life and have it abundantly' (John 10:10).

18. God's Love

For God so loved the world that he gave his only Son, that whoever believes in him should not perish but have eternal life.   John 3:16

This is really good news. God loved the people in the world so much that he worked out a plan to save them from death and hell and bring them to eternal life. God's Son came to this world as a baby called Jesus. He lived a perfect life and died to bear the punishment of the sins of whoever believes in him.

Look at the text above: John 3:16.

Write the initial letter of word number: 2 11 12 20 23 24

— — — — — —

19. A New Creation

If anyone is in Christ, he is a new creation.
2 Corinthians 5:17

When someone trusts in the Lord Jesus Christ, life changes. The person who was dead in sin, is made alive – a new creation. God gives him or her a new heart that wants to

obey God. This is a wonderful gift from God – such good news for us.

Jesus described this changed life as being born again (John 3:7). A person has to be born again to enter the kingdom of heaven.

20. Knowledge of the Truth

God desires all people to be saved and to come to the knowledge of the truth.
1 Timothy 2:4

Jesus is the truth. God wants us to be saved and to really know Jesus, not just know about him.

To really know Jesus and have him as our friend, we need to spend time with him, speaking to him in prayer and listening to what he has to say to us in the Scriptures, the Bible.

Just as we love spending time with our friends, we will love spending time with Jesus. What good news to know that he is our friend.

21. God's Grace

If only I may finish my course and the ministry that I received from the Lord Jesus, to testify to the gospel of the grace of God.
Acts 20:24

For by grace you have been saved through faith. And this is not your own doing; it is the gift of God, not a result of works, so that no one may boast.
Ephesians 2:8-9

The gospel is not a privilege that we earn. It is a gift given to us because of God's grace. A way to remember the meaning of grace is:

G Gifts
R Received
A At
C Christ's
E Expense

We have done nothing to deserve God's kindness. We are saved by grace, through faith – this is not our own doing, it is the gift of God (see Ephesians 2:8).

22. The Gospel brings Life

Our Saviour Christ Jesus, abolished death and brought life and immortality to light through the gospel.
2 Timothy 1:10

One of the gifts the gospel brings to us is eternal life.

Death was a consequence of Adam's disobedience in the Garden of Eden.

Jesus Christ, God's Son, gained the victory over death by dying on the cross and rising again on the third day.

Jesus Christ's obedience brought life for us – the life that God intended for Adam. All of life became different. Everything is in our Saviour's control.

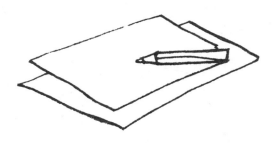

23. God Reigns

How beautiful upon the mountains are the feet of him who brings good news, who publishes peace, who brings good news of happiness, who publishes salvation, who says to Zion, 'Your God reigns.'
Isaiah 52:7

The world is full of problems – war and disease and hunger in many places. There is chaos and trouble all over.

But we have good news – 'your God reigns'.

God is in control. He upholds the whole universe by the word of his power (Hebrews 1:3).

The whole of earth and heaven belong to him (Deuteronomy 10:14). He is the King of kings. In all events and with all people, God is working out his purposes.

That should give us comfort and confidence to face the future.

24. The Gospel is Eternal

Then I (John) saw another angel flying directly overhead, with an eternal gospel to proclaim to those who dwell on earth, to every nation and tribe and language and people.
Revelation 14:6

Many of the things we value today will be gone in a few years. The toys will be broken; the bike will be

rusty; our friends might move on to a new town.

One thing we can be sure will remain constant is the Word of God. People will die. Heaven and earth will pass away. But God's Word will be forever. The gospel will last for all eternity. Those who are trusting Jesus have joy now and everlasting joy in the future.

This is good news.

25. The Gospel came in Power and Holy Spirit

Our gospel came to you not only in word, but also in power and in the Holy Spirit and with full conviction.

1 Thessalonians 1:5

The gospel is not just a collection of words on a page. The Word of God is not like any other book.

The words of the gospel are powerful because the Holy Spirit opens our minds and hearts to understand and receive the truth.

A Christian believes the gospel because of the work of God, the Holy Spirit, in his or her life.

26. The Gospel for all Nations

And the gospel must first be proclaimed to all nations.
Mark 13:10

The gospel is for you, but not just for you. It is for people all over the world. Jesus told his disciples to preach the gospel to all nations.

God's Word – the gospel – is being translated into more and more languages. Missionaries are taking the gospel to many different countries.

Is there someone you can tell about the Lord Jesus?

27. The Gospel never Changes

The word of the Lord remains forever. And this word is the good news that was preached to you.
1 Peter 1:25

The good news of the gospel never changes. It is true for us today just as it was in the past. We know

that this good news will be true in the future too, because it is the Word of God.

How thankful we should be that we have heard this good news - good news for today and every day of our lives. This helps us in times of difficulty or sadness.

28. Jesus preached the Gospel

Jesus came into Galilee, proclaiming the gospel of God.
Mark 1:14

Wherever Jesus went, he did good. He healed sick people, made blind people see and lame people walk.

He also preached the gospel wherever he went, telling people the good news of God's love for sinners and his plan to save them from eternal punishment. He knew he was going to die on the cross to carry out this plan.

29. The Gospel is to be Shared

Then Philip opened his mouth and ... he told him the good news about Jesus.
Acts 8:35

When we hear good news – perhaps the birth of a baby or someone passing an exam – we want to pass it on to others.

We should want to pass on the very good news about Jesus to our friends.

Some people become missionaries and go to foreign lands to tell people about Jesus.

Faithful ministers pass on the good news of the gospel when they preach in church week by week.

30. The Gospel is to be Believed

The time is fulfilled, and the kingdom of God is at hand; repent and believe in the gospel.
Mark 1:15

We can read the gospel. We can listen to the gospel. We can speak about the gospel.

But the really important thing is to believe the gospel – to realise what God has done for us and to thank him for sending His Son to save us. When we turn from sin and believe the gospel, we are saying 'yes' to Jesus.

From the Author

The gospel is a multi-faceted jewel which should fascinate us and rejoice our heart. In this little book we have some definitions of the gospel, some of the benefits and gifts that the gospel brings to us.

Paul in his letter to the Philippians tells us that the most important thing in his life is 'knowing Christ Jesus'. Everything else is worthless compared to that great gift of 'gaining Christ' (Philippians 3:8).

Along with all the benefits – forgiveness of sin, eternal life, help of the Holy Spirit and many others – the Christian gains the supreme gift – Christ himself.

What good news.

Carine Mackenzie

BOOKS IN THE SERIES

My 1st Book of Bible Prayers, Philip Ross
ISBN: 978-1-85792-944-7

My 1st Book of Bible Promises, Carine Mackenzie
ISBN: 978-1-84550-039-9

My 1st Book of Christian Values, Carine Mackenzie
ISBN: 978-1-84550-262-1

My 1st Book of Memory Verses, Carine Mackenzie
ISBN: 978-1-85792-783-2

My 1st Book about the Church, Carine Mackenzie
ISBN: 978-1-84550-570-7

My 1st Book of Questions and Answers,
Carine Mackenzie
ISBN: 978-1-85792-570-8

My 1st Book about Jesus, Carine Mackenzie
ISBN: 978-1-84550-463-2

My 1st Book about the Bible, Carine Mackenzie
ISBN: 978-1-78191-123-5

My 1st Book about God, Carine Mackenzie
ISBN: 978-1-78191-260-7

My 1st Book about the Gospel, Carine Mackenzie
ISBN: 978-1-78191-276-8

CHRISTIAN FOCUS PUBLICATIONS

Christian Focus Christian Heritage CF4K Mentor

Christian Focus Publications publishes books for adults and children under its four main imprints: Christian Focus, CF4K, Mentor and Christian Heritage. Our books reflect our conviction that God's Word is reliable and Jesus is the way to know him, and live for ever with him.

Our children's publication list includes a Sunday School curriculum that covers pre-school to early teens, and puzzle and activity books. We also publish personal and family devotional titles, biographies and inspirational stories that children will love.

If you are looking for quality Bible teaching for children then we have an excellent range of Bible stories and age-specific theological books.

From pre-school board books to teenage apologetics, we have it covered!

Find us at our web page:
www.christianfocus.com

CF4•K
Because you're never too young to know Jesus